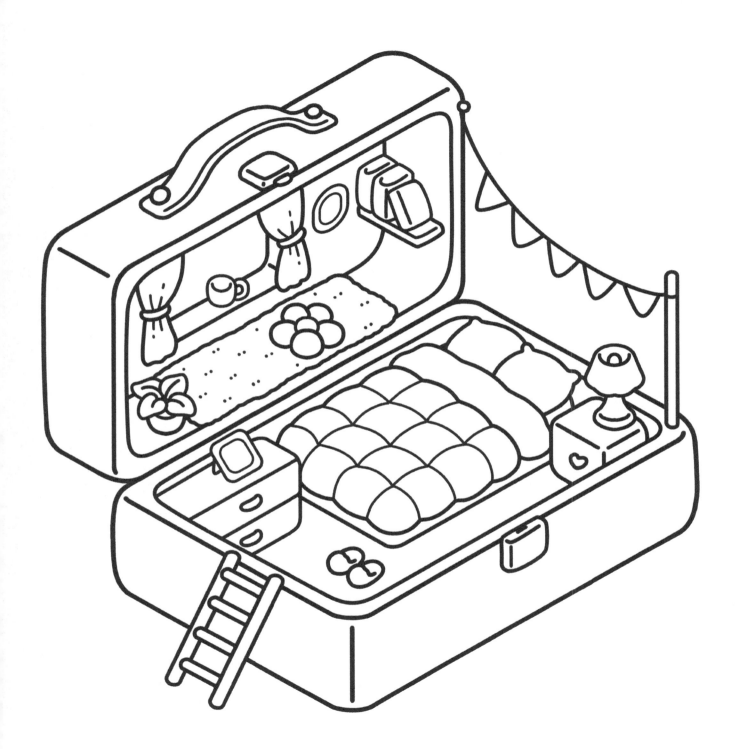

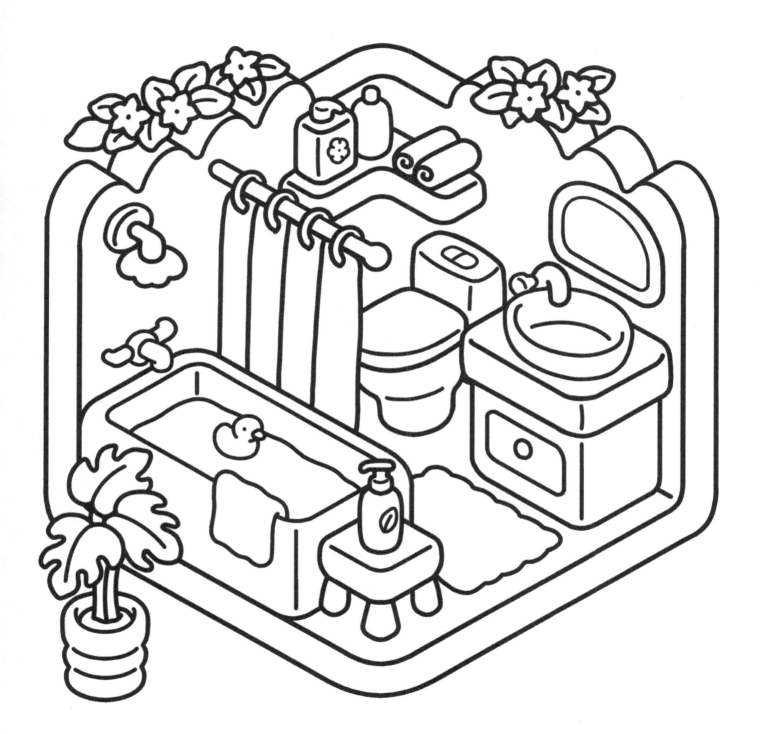

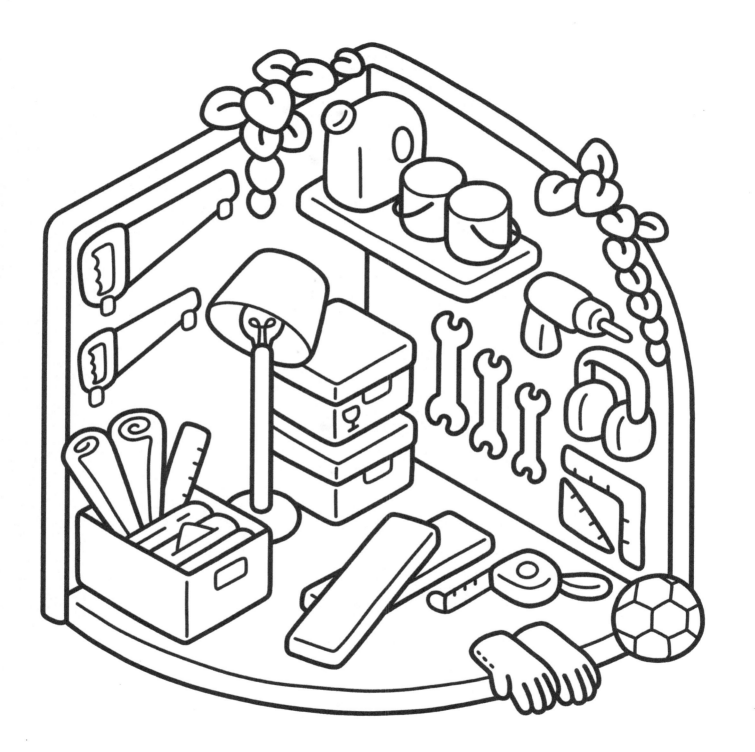

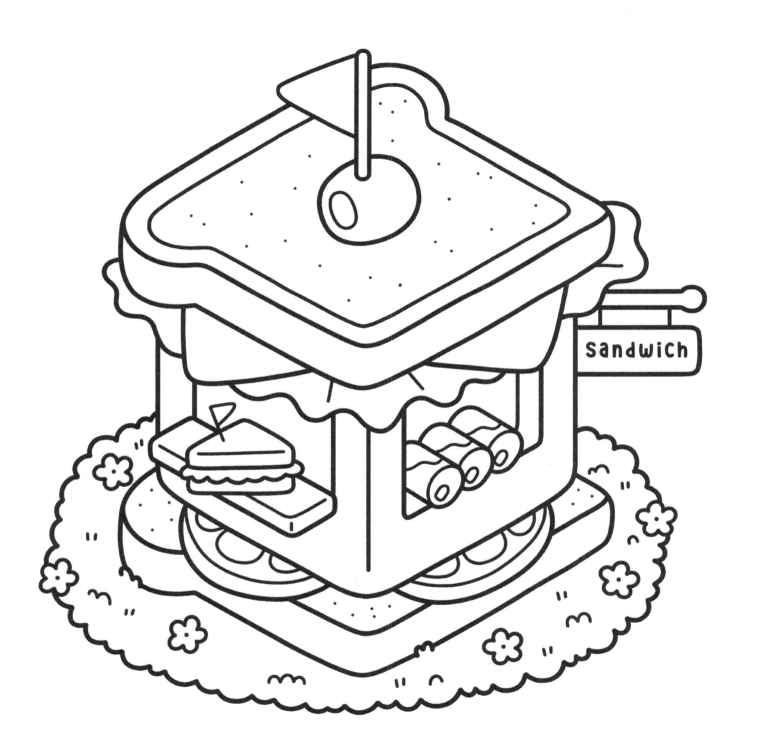

TEST COLOR PAGE

TEST COLOR PAGE

Special gift from Girl Spaces Coloring Book

Special gift from Ocean Home Coloring Book

Special gift from Xmas Corner Coloring Book

Special gift from Xmas Corner Coloring Book

Made in the USA
Coppell, TX
04 May 2025

48877976R00057